THE JACOBY & MEYERS GUIDE
TO SMALL CLAIMS LITIGATION

**Other books in the
Jacoby & Meyers Series**

GUIDE TO
SMALL
CLAIMS
LITIGATION

GAIL J. KOFF, Esquire

An Owl Book

HENRY HOLT AND COMPANY
NEW YORK

Copyright © 1991 by Jamko Service Corporation
All rights reserved, including the right to reproduce
this book or portions thereof in any form.
Published by Henry Holt and Company, Inc.,
115 West 18th Street, New York, New York 10011.
Published in Canada by Fitzhenry & Whiteside Limited,
195 Allstate Parkway, Markham, Ontario L3R 4T8.

Library of Congress Cataloging-in-Publication Data
Koff, Gail J.
The Jacoby & Meyers guide to small claims litigation /
Gail J. Koff. — 1st ed.
p.   cm.
"An Owl book."
Includes index.
ISBN 0-8050-1164-1
1. Small claims courts—United States—Popular works.   I. Title.
II. Title: Jacoby and Meyers guide to small claims litigation.
III. Title: Guide to small claims litigation.
KF8769.Z9K64   1991
347.73′04—dc20
[347.3074]   91-11232
                                     CIP

Henry Holt books are available at special discounts
for bulk purchases for sales promotions, premiums,
fund-raising, or educational use. Special editions
or book excerpts can also be created to specification.
For details contact:
Special Sales Director, Henry Holt and Company, Inc.,
115 West 18th Street, New York, New York 10011.

First Edition

Printed in the United States of America
Recognizing the importance of preserving the written word,
Henry Holt and Company, Inc., by policy, prints all of its
first editions on acid-free paper. ∞

1   3   5   7   9   10   8   6   4   2

CONTENTS

ABOUT JACOBY & MEYERS

In 1972 a survey conducted by the American Bar Association found that nearly 70 percent of the population in this country did not have adequate access to the legal system. High fees, complicated jargon, and intimidating settings were just some of the obstacles.

We established the law firm of Jacoby & Meyers to make the law accessible to what is referred to as the middle-income "legal niche." Over the eighteen years Jacoby & Meyers has been in existence, the firm has been a leader in efforts to make quality legal representation available to everyone, regardless of economic or social stratum.

In 1977, after the U.S. Supreme Court ruled that lawyers were allowed to advertise, Jacoby & Meyers became the first firm to advertise on television, making it a pioneer in the retailing of personal legal services.

Today Jacoby & Meyers is one of the largest law firms in the country. Composed of 130 firm-owned branch offices in six states (Arizona, California, Connecticut, New Jersey, New York, and Pennsylvania), it has 34 partners and 200 associate attorneys. Each year the firm gives general advice or provides specific legal services to 150,000 new clients in such areas as family law, bankruptcy, criminal law, and personal injury.

One aim of the firm has always been to educate the consumer as to how the law works. This is important for two reasons: so that consumers are able to choose the best possible representation, and also so that they can become the best possible clients for attorneys. To this end, Jacoby & Meyers is pleased to introduce this series of legal guides on specific subjects, such as *The Jacoby & Meyers Guide to Small Claims Litigation*. By presenting each subject in a clear and readable manner, it is hoped that the legal process itself will be demystified and that the reader will be given a sense of empowerment over his or her life.

Costs for legal services in this country are, as a rule, high. As a result, in cases involving only small amounts of money—under $2,500—it may not be worthwhile to hire an attorney. And yet the consumer is still entitled to legal relief. Small Claims Court was especially designed to handle cases dealing with smaller amounts of money by permitting a plaintiff to appear without being represented by an attorney.

The goal of the *Jacoby & Meyers Guide to Small Claims Litigation* is not only to advise consumers as to how to sue in Small Claims Court by setting forth the procedures and rules that apply, but also to offer concrete advice concerning courtroom strategies and how to defend themselves if they're being sued.

INTRODUCTION

One of the great advantages of our legal system is that every citizen has the right *and* the opportunity to have an injustice, no matter how small it might be, redressed.

Unfortunately, however, the costs of legal assistance in this country have risen dramatically over the years. As a result it may not always be economically feasible to retain an attorney at the possible cost of thousands of dollars to go to court to recover several hundred, or even a couple of thousand, dollars you may feel is rightfully owed you.

For instance, let's say you've recently moved out of an apartment and your landlord has refused to return your $500 security and cleaning deposit. When you ask why, he says that you left the apartment in much worse shape than when you took possession of it, and therefore you failed to live up to the terms of your lease. Your security deposit, he says, will be used to pay for the cleaning of the apartment.

But you believe that you've done a more than adequate job of cleaning the apartment—in fact, you've left it in even better shape than you found it—and so you should be entitled to a full return of your money.

To hire an attorney and take your landlord to court in

order to force him to return your deposit would probably cost you far more than the $500 he's holding on to. So, you're in a bind. Do you hire an attorney, who will probably charge you at least $1,000 to take your case, twice as much as your claim would be? Or do you simply chalk it up to the cost of renting an apartment and just walk away?

Well, you could certainly do either of these things, but you don't have to. If you truly believe that you're in the right, and you believe that the facts of the case, when properly presented, speak for themselves, then a remedy is available that is both affordable and relatively quick.

In fact, Small Claims Court was designed just for cases like these, situations in which relatively modest amounts of money are involved. The surprisingly simple procedure of going to Small Claims Court affords average citizens the opportunity to avail themselves of the legal system and obtain justice without long delays and minus the formal rules of evidence that would apply under other circumstances.

There are several advantages to Small Claims Court. For one thing, it allows you to argue disputes that involve, on the average, $2,500 or less without having to get an attorney involved (though most jurisdictions allow attorneys to appear, a few actually prohibit their appearance).

For another, bringing your dispute to Small Claims Court is a relatively simple matter. There are no complicated legal forms to fill out, and when you do appear before a judge you do not have to know what the relevant theory of law pertaining to your case is, nor will you have to be conversant with various legal procedures. Instead, you need only present the facts of your case to the best of your ability.

And finally, unlike the normal court case, which can take from two to five years to find its way into the courtroom, disputes brought to Small Claims Court are resolved quickly. In fact, most cases are heard within two months from the time the complaint is filed. And the hearing itself rarely takes more than ten or fifteen minutes, with the judge's decision (there is no jury) coming either immediately following the hearing or certainly within two or three days afterward.

At Jacoby & Meyers, we have always dedicated ourselves to providing first-rate legal assistance to the average consumer at a fair and affordable price. Nevertheless, there are times when we advise clients that it would be in their best interests to take a dispute to Small Claims Court, where they will get a fair hearing without having to run up high legal bills.

For this reason, we believe that it's important for you to know how the Small Claims Court system in this country works, how you can make it work for you, what kinds of cases you can bring, and what you can expect if you do choose to avail yourself of it.

The purpose of this book is to help familiarize consumers with the Small Claims Court system. Even though this book offers a comprehensive overview of the system, Small Claims Court procedures are established by laws of the individual states. Therefore, some of the specifics regarding procedures, monetary limits, rules concerning who can and can't sue and who you can sue, and the kinds of papers that must be filed throughout the different steps of the process vary from state to state. If you are considering taking your case to Small Claims Court, be sure to contact your local court for a list of rules and procedures.

1

HOW TO AVOID
SMALL CLAIMS COURT

Before you decide it's time to take your case to Small
Claims Court, you should have exhausted every effort to
settle amicably. No matter how simple it is to utilize Small
Claims Court, there is still a certain amount of time and
trouble involved, as well as the risk that you may either lose
your case or that the judge will not award you the full
amount of money you're seeking. Additionally, for some
people going to court exacts a psychological toll—for them,
getting up in front of a judge might be an emotional night-
mare. And then, even if you win, *you* are still responsible
for collecting your judgment; if your adversary decides to
make things difficult for you, this can mean even more time,
trouble, and money (for marshal's fees, for instance).

For these reasons, you should make every effort to settle
your dispute before you decide to sue.

Compromise

Your first step should be to contact the person or business
with whom you're having the dispute and try to work things
out. Calmly discuss the matter, giving your side of the

dispute and listening to the other side's argument. If they can't convince you and you can't convince them, see if you can come up with some kind of compromise that's acceptable to you both. You may not receive everything you believe you're entitled to, but, in the long run, you may be far better off than if you have to go to court.

If you are able to come up with some kind of acceptable compromise settlement, it's a good idea to get it in writing, perhaps in the form of a release. This way, if there is a problem down the line, you will have proof of the settlement.

The Demand Letter

If this attempt at compromise fails, you may decide to drop the matter completely, or you may decide to move on to the next step, which is to write what is commonly referred to as a *demand letter*. Some states even go so far as to require that just such a letter be sent before you file a court action.

The letter should be brief—no longer than two pages—and get right to the point. Set forth your case *politely*, *rationally*, and *logically*, giving the pertinent facts of the dispute and what you expect to be compensated for. You should also mention that if you do not get satisfaction, you will be forced to take the matter to court. Put in a time limit. Don't make it sound like a threat, but rather a reluctantly taken last resort. Send two copies—one by regular mail and one by certified mail, return receipt requested.

A sample letter might look something like this:

Dear Sir:

    On August 2, 1990, you agreed to pay me $550 to paint your apartment. Two days later I received a check from you in the amount of $200, which was to act as a deposit, and the rest was payable when the job was completed. On August 6, I began work and two weeks later, on August 20, the job was completed. Since then I have called and asked for my money several times, and each time I was told that payment would be forthcoming.

It is now November and I have still not received payment for the $350 you still owe me. Perhaps it is merely due to an oversight, but in any case I would appreciate it if you would remit the $350 immediately.

If I do not receive your check within ten days, I will be forced to bring the matter to court.

Sincerely,

As you can see, the letter is firm, polite, to the point, and it conveys to your adversary that you are ready to take legal steps in order to get what's owed you.

Be sure to keep a copy of this letter because if no settlement or compromise is forthcoming, it will be part of the evidence that you present in Small Claims Court.

If, after receiving this letter, your adversary still refuses to settle, you will have to decide whether court action is in your best interests.

If you do decide to sue, you can still settle after you've filed in Small Claims Court or even up to right before your case is called before the judge. (Your adversary might not think you're serious about suing until he or she is actually served with the papers and only then will he or she try to settle.) If this happens, simply inform the judge that you've come to a fair settlement, how much it's for, and how it is to be paid, either in a lump sum or over a period of time. The judge then can dismiss the case, if the sum is paid at the time, or he or she can enter a judgment for the amount that's been decided upon, if payment is to be made at a later date.

If you do settle, draw up an agreement or, as it's called,

a *stipulation*. Include in this stipulation a clause that obliges the party who owes you money to agree that if he or she defaults, you can enter a judgment or go straight to the marshal who will collect what's due you. For a stipulation such as this, it's a good idea to consult an attorney.

Mediation

A growing trend in the legal field is having people settle their disputes by discussing them with a trained mediator. The idea is to present the dispute to an impartial person who will then try to come up with a fair compromise. A handful of states actually encourage this form of mediation, which takes place before an attorney, trained in the art of arbitration, who has volunteered to be an arbitrator. This procedure may cut the time that it would take for your case to be heard in Small Claims Court. In some states that offer arbitration as an option to Small Claims Court, the parties must agree that the decision reached by the arbitrator is final and may not be appealed—New York is one such state. In other states this kind of arbitration is nonbinding, and, if the attempt fails, the case may still be brought to Small Claims Court.

Five Most Commonly Asked Questions

1. *At what point should I consider taking someone to Small Claims Court?*

   Only after you have exhausted every effort to come to an amicable settlement. Talk to the person with whom you're having the dispute in a rational, measured way. Don't be accusatory and don't lose your temper. Try to see his or her side of the argument. If this fails, then you should certainly consider Small Claims Court.

2. *If I have a dispute with someone and we are able to come to an equitable settlement, how can I be sure that he follows through on it? And if he doesn't, is there any way I can protect myself?*

Any settlement you make should be put in writing. If you do settle, make sure that it's spelled out specifically in any agreement how payment is to be made, over how much time, and when each payment is due. If the agreement is not lived up to, you then have the option of taking the matter to Small Claims Court. Your signed agreement will become part of the evidence you present to the judge. It may be beneficial to have an attorney prepare the agreement, to make sure that all your rights are protected.

3. *I'm having a dispute with a local dress shop and I'm not good in face-to-face confrontations. Is there any way I can try to settle this dispute short of taking it to Small Claims Court, without talking to the people involved?*

Try what's called a demand letter. In this letter, which should be no longer than two pages, state the facts of the case, your position, and what you would accept as a settlement. As with any negotiation, it's a good idea to start with a somewhat higher figure. Be polite, not adversarial. Mention that if you do not get satisfaction, you will be forced to take the matter to Small Claims Court. If this doesn't get any action, you will have to consider doing just that. Remember to keep a copy of the letter, just in case you do have to go to court.

4. *Once I've filed in Small Claims Court, does this mean I can no longer settle the case myself?*

You can always settle the case yourself, even up to the minute before you appear in court. In fact, most judges will insist that you try to settle before the case is brought before the court.

5. *My state offers the option of mediation. Should I try it?*

It might not be a bad idea. It's a way to settle your case without having to go to court, which will save you some time. Find out, though, whether the arbitrator's decision is binding and unappealable, or whether if you're not satisfied with the decision you still have the right to take the matter to court.

2

TO SUE OR NOT TO SUE

The first thing you must decide before you initiate the process to bring your dispute to Small Claims Court is whether or not it's worth the effort.

For instance, let's say you bring a shirt to your local laundry. During the laundering process the shirt is ripped in several places. The owner of the establishment refuses to reimburse you for the shirt, maintaining that it was already torn when you brought it in. You argue that it wasn't and, when he won't give in, you threaten to bring him to Small Claims Court to recover the value of the shirt. He dares you to go ahead and do it.

Should you?

The answer is probably not. Let's say the value of the shirt when new was $50. But you've worn it several times. Thus the value of the shirt has decreased substantially (we'll talk about this later, but briefly you would not be entitled to the replacement value of the shirt, but rather its fair market value at the time it was destroyed).

You could take the matter to Small Claims Court, but what would you gain? Even if the court decided that you were entitled to $25 in damages, would this be worth your time and effort, not to mention the small filing fee you'd have to make? (In some states, court costs are awarded to the winner.) What it might boil down to is this: Is the principle of the matter worth the trouble you'd have to go through?

Too Complicated for Small Claims Court?

Generally speaking, no case is too complicated to be brought to Small Claims Court. Instead, the decision is usually an economic one. If the case is worth less than $250, it just doesn't make economic sense to bring the matter to Small Claims Court.

Basically, the kinds of cases likely to be found in Small Claims Court include:

1. Landlord-tenant
2. Property damage
3. Disputes over services rendered
4. Personal injury cases (as long as the damages fall under the Small Claims Court limit)
5. Contract disputes

Can You Collect?

Another question you'll have to address before making the decision to take your dispute to Small Claims Court is whether you will be able to collect anything from the defendant if you win.

For instance, let's say a neighbor visits your home one day and playfully tosses an expensive vase in the air. You ask him to stop, but he doesn't. His attention is distracted when your wife comes in the room, and the vase falls to the ground and breaks into pieces. Your neighbor refuses to replace the vase or pay you a fair price for its value.

Certainly, the facts of the case indicate that your neighbor was negligent in his handling of the object, but should you sue for the $1,000 that the vase was worth?

Under most circumstances, the answer might be yes. But what if your neighbor has been out of work for six months due to a physical disability, has very few prospects of getting work in the foreseeable future, and has virtually no assets? Even if you win the case, how could you possibly collect the damages? Consequently, you'd either have to wait until a later time when your neighbor might have the assets to pay off a judgment (remember that you must file within the appropriate statute of limitations—the time period under which you have to make your claim—or your case will be dismissed), or you can just forget the whole thing.

In deciding whether to sue you ought to do a little checking on the potential defendant's ability to pay if you win your case. For instance, does he or she have a history of voluntarily paying debts? Does he or she have a job? Does he or she have other means of support, or nonexempt assets that you may attach, such as a bank account or real property (excluding the home in which he or she lives)? If you are suing a business, you must make sure it is solvent and has the reputation of paying off debts.

Besides the questions of whether it's financially worthwhile to sue and whether the defendant has the means to pay off a judgment, there are other matters that should also be taken into consideration before you decide to use Small Claims Court.

You must, for instance, be certain that the amount of your claim is not in excess of the Small Claims Court maximum (unless, of course, you choose to waive the difference and sue for less, which you may do).

You must be certain that you bring your suit within the appropriate statue of limitations.

You must be sure to bring the suit in the proper jurisdictional court.

And finally, you must make sure that you are suing the proper party. For instance, if you're in automobile accident, do you sue the driver or the registered owner of the car? The answer is, both.

Have You Got a Case?

Of primary importance, of course, is the question of whether you've actually got a case. The mere fact that you've suffered a monetary loss doesn't necessarily mean that you are entitled to recovery. You must be able to prove to the satisfaction of a judge that the person you are suing is, indeed, responsible for that loss and should be held legally accountable. In other words, you must prove that the person's wrongful conduct led to your monetary loss.

The vase incident is a good example. Your neighbor was certainly negligent in tossing it around, and the fact that he refused to stop when you asked him to reinforces your case. Therefore, his behavior most certainly led to the destruction of the vase. The vase was worth $1,000 (as a collectible, it wouldn't depreciate), and so you can sue for that amount (you will, of course, not only have to prove that your neighbor was negligent, which you might do by calling your wife as a witness, but also have some expert attest to the value of the vase). An expert might be too expensive. In that case, most states will allow two appraisals or the paid receipt for the item.

What You Can Sue For

If you have experienced a monetary loss, you may sue, but your suit should fit into one of the following legal categories.

1. The negligent acts of the person you are suing must have resulted in some property damage that can be translated into a monetary loss. The vase incident is a good example of a matter that would fit into this category, because your neighbor did not act with reasonable care when it came to handling the object.

2. Due either to the intentional or negligent behavior of the person you are suing, you have suffered some kind of personal injury. Perhaps, instead of that vase, your neighbor tosses around an iron statue, which slips from his hand, falls on your foot, and breaks your toe. You might sue for the medical bills, plus any uncompensated time you're forced to miss work.

3. A valid contract signed by both parties is broken and, as a result, you suffer a monetary loss. This contract may be written, oral, or implied. For instance, let's say you're a freelance artist and you're hired by someone to design a company logo, for which you are to receive $500. When you submit your design, your employer rejects it and refuses to pay. You may take the employer to Small Claims Court and sue him or her for the $500, plus court costs, because an oral contract was breached.

4. Injury is due to a defective product, which would allow you to collect damages under the doctrine of strict liability. For instance, if you buy a can of hair spray and, due to a defective nozzle, you can't shut the spray off and it accidentally ignites, the company that produced the hair spray would be liable for damages.

5. Legislative acts sometimes create rights, such as consumer protection laws. If these rights are violated, resulting in some kind of monetary loss, you may be entitled to recover. This would include cases of false and deceptive advertising. The bait-and-switch gambit is a good example. Here a store advertises a ridiculously low price on an item to get you into the store and then informs you that that item is either unavailable or junk that will fall apart after

limited use. At this point, you receive a high-powered sales pitch to purchase a much more expensive model.

6. Merchants often extend written or implied warranties. If these warranties are breached and you suffer monetary losses, you may be entitled to recovery. This would include warranties on items such as cars, stereos, televisions, kitchen appliances, and the like. It also includes implied warranties of general fitness for products. For instance, if you purchase a toaster, you have every right to believe that it will perform the function it was made for, that is, toasting bread. If it doesn't, then even without an explicit warranty, you still have the right to recover.

Even though your case should fit into one of these categories, one of the advantages of Small Claims Court is that you yourself don't have to argue the theory of law on which recovery might be based. Instead, you simply present the facts of the case to the judge, offer proof that you have sustained an actual monetary loss, convince the court that you are suing the proper person, and then let the judge decide who's in the right.

Five Most Commonly Asked Questions

1. *Six months ago I lent a friend $60, and he has made no attempt to pay me back. Should I take him to Small Claims Court?*

   You could, but before you do perhaps you ought to weigh what's involved and then decide whether it's worth your while. You have to file the proper papers (which includes paying a small fee), gather evidence that your friend does, indeed, owe you the money, then appear in court. If the decision goes your way, you are then responsible for collecting the judgment. And then you run the risk of losing this person's friendship. Is it worth it for $60? Only you can make that decision.

2. *An acquaintance borrowed my stereo, which is worth over $1,000, and then broke it beyond repair. He refuses to pay for it, and part of his argument is that he doesn't have any money. Should I bring him to Small Claims Court?*

If your friend does not, indeed, have any money, there may be little point in bringing him to Small Claims Court. Even if you win a judgment, what are you going to collect? This is one of the things you have to take into consideration before deciding to file in Small Claims Court: the ability of your adversary to pay in the event that you win. In this case, it appears to be a waste of time.

3. *We were having a party at my house and a guest accidentally broke a lamp. Can I take him to Small Claims Court to recover the cost of the item?*

You would have to prove negligence on your guest's part, or that he did it intentionally, which, under the circumstances, might be very difficult to do.

4. *I purchased a dishwasher and it broke down while still under warranty. Nevertheless, I'm having a difficult time getting the manufacturer to repair the machine. Can I take them to Small Claims Court?*

You may, but first write a demand letter. If this doesn't work, the case would fall within the written warranty theory and you would have a valid case.

5. *Do I need a working knowledge of the law before taking a case to Small Claims Court?*

No. All you have to do is present the facts, and the judge will apply the appropriate law to that set of facts. However, it's in your best interests to present those facts as logically, calmly, and clearly as possible.

3

THE RULES
OF THE GAME

How Much Can You Sue For?

Each state sets the maximum amounts for which you can sue in Small Claims Court. When you get the rules from your local Small Claims Court clerk, this amount will be listed. You may not exceed it.

Following is a state-by-state listing of the maximum amounts for each state. However, as these amounts are revised periodically, be sure to get an up-to-date copy of your local rules to see if there have been any changes.

Alabama	$ 1,000
Alaska	$ 5,000
Arizona	$ 500
Arkansas	$ 3,000
California	$ 1,500
Colorado	$ 1,000
Connecticut	$ 1,500
Delaware	$ 2,500
District of Columbia	$ 2,000
Florida	$ 2,500

Georgia	$ 3,000
Hawaii	$ 2,500
Idaho	$ 2,000
Illinois	$ 2,500
Indiana	$ 3,000
Iowa	$ 2,000
Kansas	$ 1,000
Kentucky	$ 1,000
Louisiana	$ 2,000
Maine	$ 1,400
Maryland	$ 2,500
Massachusetts	$ 1,500 (no limit for action for property damage caused by a motor vehicle)
Michigan	$ 1,500
Minnesota	$ 2,000
Mississippi	$ 1,000
Missouri	$ 1,000
Montana	$ 1,500
Nebraska	$ 1,500
Nevada	$ 1,500
New Hampshire	$ 1,500
New Jersey	$ 1,000
New Mexico	$ 2,000
New York	$ 2,000
North Carolina	$ 1,500
North Dakota	$ 2,000
Ohio	$ 1,000 for claims, $ 1,500 for counter-claims
Oklahoma	$ 1,500
Oregon	$ 2,500
Pennsylvania	Municipal Court: $5,000 District Court: $4,000

Rhode Island	$ 1,500
South Carolina	$ 1,000
South Dakota	$ 2,000
Tennessee	$10,000 to $15,000
Texas	$ 1,000
Utah	$ 1,000
Vermont	$ 2,000
Virginia	$ 7,000
Washington	$ 1,000
West Virginia	$ 3,000
Wisconsin	$ 1,000
Wyoming	$ 750

When preparing your case, you must take into account your state's maximum Small Claims Court recovery figure. If your state's limit is $1,000 and your claim is for $2,500, obviously you should think twice about using Small Claims Court. On the other hand, if your claim is for $1,200 in a state where the limit is $1,000, you may decide to lower your claim to $1,000 in order to bring your dispute into Small Claims Court.

There are advantages to using the Small Claims Court system, and it may be worth your while to do so. First, you will not need an attorney, which might save you far more than the $200 you're sacrificing in the above instance. Also, Small Claims Court is quicker than the normal court system, and the time you save may easily offset the $200 you have to give up.

In some unusual circumstances you may be able to do what is called *splitting your claim*, which would allow you to sue for a higher total amount. However, to split a claim you would have to bring multiple suits against the other person, each one based on a different claim. Thus you would have to argue that the case either involves two or more separate injuries or contracts.

For instance, let's say you hire someone to repair and

then install an air conditioner. The person fails to do so properly and the amount of damage comes to over the limit allowed in Small Claims Court. You might be able to argue that there were two separate contracts, one for repairing and one for installing, and then sue on the basis of separate claims. While in most cases a judge might rule against you, forcing you to choose one of the claims, bringing both suits might be worth the gamble.

However, as the procedure is rather complicated, it's a good idea to consult an attorney.

How Much Should You Sue For?

Property Damage Cases

If property that you own is damaged by someone through either an intentional or a negligent act, you have the right to recover for any loss you sustain. Usually, this is the amount of money it would take to repair the damaged property.

For instance, if your bicycle is parked in an appropriate rack and someone comes along in a car and smashes into it, damaging the rear wheel, you would be entitled to the cost of repair for that wheel.

However, if the cost of repair to your property exceeds the actual market value of the item, you would not be entitled to the repair figure. Instead, you would be entitled to the fair market value of the bicycle at the time of the accident, not when it was new, even though you would not be able to replace the bicycle for that amount.

Personal Injury Cases

In personal injury cases you are entitled to out-of-pocket medical expenses, including necessary transportation to and from any medical care facility or doctor's office; loss of pay, or vacation time due to missed work (if, however, you have a job that provides unlimited paid sick time, you have nothing to recover); and any damage to property that might have occurred as a result of the accident. For instance, if you trip over an object that was negligently left out, you might, in addition to bodily injuries, tear a hole in your trousers.

You may also be entitled to recovery for "pain and suffering." This is a rather vague term that allows you to recover for the discomfort that comes as a result of the injury. In general, attorneys usually multiply their claims by three or four times to compute for "pain and suffering." Therefore, if your medical costs are $250, you should probably sue for $1,000. Whether you will get this much is completely up to the individual judge.

Note that unless you have documented proof of medical treatment, the chances are that a judge will not give you anything for "pain and suffering."

If you are a defendant being sued by someone for an automobile accident, you should notify your insurance company, which will handle the case for you. However, there may be some reason that you prefer to handle the matter yourself. Perhaps the amount you're being sued for is less than the deductible, or perhaps you don't want to involve your insurance company because you're afraid your rates will be raised. If that's the case, you might choose to go to Small Claims Court instead.

Breach-of-Contract Cases

The way to compute the size of your claim in breach-of-contract cases is relatively simple. Just figure out the difference between the amount you were supposed to receive under the contract and the amount you actually did receive. If there's a loan involved, don't forget to add the interest.

For example, let's say you contracted to build a bookcase

for someone for $300. You receive a downpayment of $100 but, when the job is completed, the person you did the work for refuses to pay you the rest of what's owed you, which amounts to $200. Consequently, your suit in Small Claims Court would be for $200.

Clothing Cases

When new or almost new clothing has been damaged or lost, you should sue for its cost. However, if the clothing is older, the court will probably recompense you only for the value of the clothing at the time it was lost or damaged. In other words, the leather jacket that cost $300 when you bought it new a year ago is really worth only about $150 today. That's the amount you should sue for. On the other hand, if you bought the jacket for $300 last week and it was damaged beyond repair, you can sue for the $300 cost.

When suing for damaged or lost clothing, you should be prepared to prove how much the item cost, how old it was when it was damaged or lost, and whether in its present damaged condition it still has some value to you.

When you're figuring the amount of your claim, place it a little on the high side. The judge can always lower the amount of the settlement, but he or she can't give you more than you ask for.

The Statute of Limitations

The statute of limitations is the time limit under which the suit must be brought. Each state has its own set of statutes of limitations for individual kinds of cases. But regardless of what the differences are, they will never be less than one year. (If you are suing a city, county, or state government, make sure of the rules, because some require immediate notification and the filing of what is called a Proof of Claim.)

Following is partial list of the California Statute of Limitations. Though there are some variations from state to state, the California time limitations are typical, so they will give you a good idea of what you can expect in your own jurisdiction.

1. Oral Contracts: Two years from the day the contract is broken.
2. Written Contracts: Four years from the day the contract is broken.
3. Personal Injury: One year from the date of the injury, or, if the injury is not immediately apparent, one year from the date that it is discovered.
4. Real or Personal Property Damage: Three years from the date that the damage took place.
5. Professional Negligence Against Health Care Providers: Three years after the date of the injury, or, if it is not apparent until some time later, one year from that date.
6. Fraud: Three years from the date of the discovery of the fraud.
7. Suits Against Public Agencies: Six months from the time the claim occurred.

Generally speaking, the statute of limitations starts to run either from the day a contract is broken or from the day the injury to either your property or your person occurred.

In some cases, the statute of limitations may be suspended for a period of time. This would occur if the person being sued is in prison, living out of the state, certified as being insane, or a minor. Once the appropriate situation changes, the statute of limitations starts up again.

If you are the defendant in a Small Claims case and you believe that the statute of limitations has run its course, point this out to the judge at the time of your appearance. It could mean the dismissal of your case.

Who Can Sue and Be Sued

As long as you are of legal age in your state (most states require you to be eighteen) and have not been declared mentally incompetent, you may sue in Small Claims Court.

In most states you can be represented by an attorney, but even in those states that do not allow appearances by attorneys, you may certainly seek their advice beforehand.

If you are an unemancipated minor (that is, someone under the age of eighteen who has not petitioned the court and been granted emancipation, which releases that person from a parent's custody and control), your parent or legal guardian must sue for you. In some states, even if you are emancipated, you must also have a parent or legal guardian sue for you. In others you may sue for yourself. Check the rules of your individual state.

In many states small unincorporated businesses may use Small Claims Court.

In most states you are permitted to sue persons, partnerships, corporations, and state and local governments in Small Claims Court.

Where You Can Sue

Rules on where you can sue vary from state to state. In some states you are permitted to sue another person only in the district or county in which he or she resides. In other states you are permitted to choose the place where the accident occurred, where the contract was broken or originally signed, where the merchandise was purchased, or where the corporation does business.

Because the rules vary, it's best to check your individual state. Generally speaking, however, you may sue in the following places:

1. In all states you may sue in the county where the defendant either resides or has a place of business.

2. In some states you may sue in the county where the contract for performance was signed.

3. In some states you may sue in the county where the personal injury or the property damage occurred.

4. In some states you may sue in the county where the defendant lived or did business at the time the contract was entered into.

Five Most Commonly Asked Questions

1. *I have a claim of $1,500 against an employer who hired me to build an extension on his house and then canceled the job in the middle and refused to pay me. Unfortunately, the state in which I live has a $1,000 maximum for Small Claims Court. Is there anything I can do?*

   Either you can lower your claim to $1,000, thereby forfeiting the additional $500, or you can try to figure out how to make two separate claims out of the $1,500, thereby splitting them so they fall under the maximum. Perhaps you could break down your work into two different jobs.

2. *I was in an automobile accident and the damages to my car amounted to $2,500 in order to repair it. The car itself is worth only $2,000. Can I still sue for $2,500 in Small Claims Court?*

   You can sue for $2,500, but you should be aware that if the cost of repairs is more than the fair market value of your car, you will probably only receive an amount that is the equivalent of the value of the car.

3. *I received a badly sprained ankle due to the negligence of a neighbor who left his lawnmower on the sidewalk. I lost several days' work and had to purchase medical supplies. Am I also entitled to something for "pain and suffering"?*

   You might be, but unless you received medical attention and have proof of it, you may have trouble convincing a judge that you should be recompensed for "pain and suffering." This is one reason attorneys usually advise seeking medical attention, even for something rather minor in nature.

4. *I took a dress that I purchased last year for $250 to be cleaned and it was lost. Can I sue for what I paid for the dress?*

   As the dress was a year old, you will probably have to settle for a reduced amount, perhaps half.

5. *I live in one county, the person I want to sue lives in another county, and the injury occurred in a third county. In which county am I able to sue?*

   Depending on the rules of the state in which you reside, you may be able to sue in any one or all of the jurisdictions. If you are allowed your choice, it's probably a good idea to choose the one most convenient for you.

4

TAKING YOUR CASE
TO COURT

Costs

Once you've made the decision to take your dispute to Small
Claims Court, you should obtain a copy of the rules from
the court clerk. When you've determined the proper jurisdiction, you should visit the court, pick up the appropriate
papers (which the clerk will help you fill out), and then pay
the filing fee, which is quite reasonable. The range of the
cost of filing will be from $5 to $25, and in some states this
includes mailing fees.

The only other court cost you will encounter is a small
fee for serving papers on the defendant. However, many
states allow personal service, which a friend or relative may
do without charge.

How to Fill Out the
Court Papers

The court papers themselves are really quite simple to
complete. But if you do have any trouble filling them out,
you may obtain help from the Small Claims Court clerk.

Some states even have trained legal assistants who will answer any questions you might have.

Although the papers might differ somewhat depending on the state, for the most part they are rather similar. The following general explanation should suffice no matter which state you file in.

The first form you will be asked to fill out is called the Plaintiff's Statement, or Statement of Claim, depending on your local court.

If you are suing one person, simply name him or her by the most complete name that you have. For instance, if you know the person only by the first initials and the last name, such as C. P. Phillips, refer to him that way, or if you only know him by a nickname—Chip Jackson, perhaps—use that. However, in order to avoid delays and improper or invalid service, make every effort to name correctly the party or company that you intend to sue.

If you are suing more than one person, be sure to list each one properly by the most complete name that you have. Even if you are suing a husband and wife, you must name them both.

If you are suing an individually owned business, make sure that you name the business properly, not simply by using the owner's name, though you may use his or her name as well.

If you are suing a partnership, make sure that you list the names of all the partners, not just an individual. The reason for this is that in a business partnership, all partners are individually liable to all the acts of the business.

If you're suing a corporation, give the full name of the corporation. You should not sue individuals in the corporation, such as the officers (unless you have a specific personal claim against them), but rather the corporation as a whole.

If you are suing as a result of a motor vehicle accident, you should name both the driver of the vehicle and the

INSTRUCTIONS:
Place only ONE letter or number in each space and leave a blank space between words.

CIVIL COURT OF THE CITY OF NEW YORK
SMALL CLAIMS PART
STATEMENT OF CLAIM

(FOR OFFICE USE ONLY)

SC#

CERT'D #

TODAY'S DATE

COA CODE

CLAIM AMT.
$

FEE
STANDARD FEE PLUS POSTAGE
☐ CLAIMANT V. DEFENDANT
☐ DEFENDANT V. THIRD PARTY
NO FEE. POSTAGE ONLY
☐ CLAIMANT V. ADD'L DEFENDANT
☐ WAGE CLAIM TO $300
RECEIPT #

LANGUAGE

DATE DATA ENTERED

DATE NOTICES MAILED

CASE TYPE:
MULTI DFT ☐   CTR/CLM ☐
3 PARTY ☐   CRS/CMPLT ☐

FIRST DATE

TRIAL DATE

DAY COURT
☐ STATUTORY
☐ OTHER

I CLAIMANT'S INFORMATION

(Your)
LAST NAME
FIRST NAME   MIDDLE INITIAL
ADDRESS
BOROUGH   STATE   ZIP
OTHER INFO
(Doing Business As
or In Care Of)
PHONE NO. (   )

II DEFENDANT'S INFORMATION

(Their)
LAST NAME
(or business name)
FIRST NAME   MIDDLE INITIAL
ADDRESS
BOROUGH   STATE   ZIP
OTHER INFO
(Doing Business As
or In Care Of)
PHONE NO. (   )

III CLAIM

Amount Claimed: $_____ (Maximum $2,000)   Date of Occurrence or Accident:_____

Briefly state your claim here:
_____
_____
_____

If Automobile Accident (Note: Claim must be Owner against Owner.)

License Plate Number of Defendant's Car:_____   State:_____

Place of Occurrence of Accident:_____

Today's Date _____   Signature of Claimant or Agent _____

(FOR OFFICE USE ONLY)

CIV-SC-50 (Revised 7/89)

registered owner. If the driver was on the job at the time, you may also want to sue his or her employer.

Often there are special rules when it comes to suing government agencies. Consequently, you should ask the Small Claims Court for these rules and the specific procedures you must follow.

It is very important that you make sure that you've chosen the proper judicial district to sue in and that you have named the defendant properly.

Filing the Papers

When you complete the Plaintiff's Statement, submit it to the county clerk. Depending on the state in which you're filing, the clerk will either file it directly or retype it and then assign you a case number. You will then be asked to sign this second form, with a warning that if there are any known untruths you will be subject to a penalty for perjury. One copy of what is now known as the Claim of Plaintiff (depending on the court's procedures) will go to the judge and another must be served on the defendant.

Next the clerk will ask you about a court date. Many states have specific rules as to when the court date must be held after filing the proper papers, while others simply require an "early" hearing.

Although most Small Claims Courts are held on weekdays, starting at 9 o'clock in the morning, some jurisdictions do hold sessions in the evenings or on Saturdays.

Set a date that is convenient for you and that will allow you enough time to serve the papers on the defendant.

If you are a defendant in a Small Claims case, normally you do not have to file any papers. All you need to do is show up on the date and time indicated on the Plaintiff's Claim. If, for some reason, you cannot appear on the date named, first call the plaintiff and ask him or her to change it to a more convenient day. If the plaintiff is uncooperative, simply write a letter to the clerk of the Small Claims Court, giving the complaint number, the name of the plaintiff, and the date of the hearing. Make sure your letter reaches the clerk before your court date or else a default judgment might be issued against you. Inform the clerk that you have already tried to change the date with the plaintiff, but he or she has been uncooperative, and then give the reason why you cannot attend at the named date. Finally, offer a series of dates when you can attend. For instance, you might say that you can make the hearing anytime after October 22 but never on Tuesdays.

If you are the defendant and the plaintiff agrees to change the date, still either send a letter to the court prior to the first scheduled date or have a friend or relative appear to make sure that the case has been adjourned.

In some cases you may, as a defendant, wish to file a counterclaim that arises from the same incident as the plaintiff's case. In some jurisdictions you may be permitted to do this orally when the case is called; in other states you must state your counterclaim in writing. If this is the case, you must go to Small Claims Court and obtain a defendant's counterclaim form.

Serving the Papers

Once you've filled out the appropriate papers, a copy must be served on the defendant, whether it is a person(s), corporation, or partnership. Failure to accomplish this *service of process*, which gives those you are suing notification of the nature of your claim and the day, time, and place of the hearing, means that your suit has not been properly started.

If you have named more than one defendant on your

Claim of Plaintiff, then *each* defendant must be served (this includes serving husband and wife separately, if you have named them separately—it doesn't matter if they live together, they must still be served individually).

As a rule, you must serve the defendant within the state where your action is brought. For instance, you can't sue someone in New York and serve papers on him or her in New Jersey (the one general exception is concerning motor vehicle accidents, for which many states have out-of-state service procedures).

Most states allow you to serve the defendant anyplace in the state in which you have brought the action. However, some states (New York is one) generally require that the defendant be served in the same county or judicial district in which the lawsuit was filed.

There are several ways to serve the papers, but in all cases you must know where to find the defendant. If you don't, there's no reason to go ahead with the suit, as it is not complete unless you actually serve the papers. In some states the court will take care of service.

Personal Service

1. Every state allows personal service to be made by officers of the law (police officers, marshals, sheriffs). However, there is usually a fee for this, most often $20 and up. In many states this fee or a portion of it is recoverable if you win your suit.
2. Many states allow the hiring of a private process server. In a number of states this fee or a portion of it is recoverable, if you win your suit. However, some states require that you first attempt to serve the papers yourself, before they will allow you to recover the cost of hiring a private process server to do so. Check the rules in your state to

find out if using private process servers is permissible.

3. Several states allow service by any person age eighteen or older, including friends or relatives. However, this does not include the person bringing the suit.

No matter who accomplishes the personal service, the Claim of Plaintiff must be handed to the defendant *personally*. It cannot simply be left in the mailbox or with a secretary at the defendant's place of business. For this reason, it is important that the person making the service either be familiar with the defendant or have some sure-fire way of making certain he or she is serving the right person.

If the defendant refuses to accept service, the process server should merely put the paper down and leave. Even though the papers are not physically handed to the defendant, in such cases proper service is considered to have taken place.

Service by Registered
or Certified Mail

In most states you have the option of serving papers by certified or registered mail (some states require that you try personal service first). The certified receipt card should be returned to the Court Clerk. Often, for a small fee, the court clerk will do the mailing for you (this fee is recoverable, if you win the suit).

If you do choose to serve this way, you must make sure that the defendant him- or herself signs for the letter. If he or she does not, you will have to try personal service again.

If you do use the mail, it's a good idea to call the court clerk several days before your scheduled court appearance and make sure that the service has been completed (this means that the clerk has received the appropriately signed mail receipt).

Substituted Service

If the defendant is for some reason particularly difficult to serve (according to most state rules the plaintiff must use "reasonable diligence" to serve), many states allow the plaintiff to serve by leaving a copy of the papers at the person's dwelling place in the presence of a competent member of the household, which, in many states, means that he or she must be at least eighteen years old. This person must be told what the papers are about. After this is done a copy of the papers must *also* be sent by first-class mail to the person served. Service is considered completed ten days after mailing.

Because many Small Claims Court clerks interpret the term "reasonable diligence" differently, it's a good idea to discuss the situation with the clerk before you try this method.

After this kind of service is completed, you must return a Proof of Service form to the clerk, attesting that all proper "service" steps have been successfully completed.

Obviously, the defendant is entitled to receive service of the Claim of Plaintiff before the date of the court hearing. Each state has a rule as to how much notice the defendant is entitled to (some require as many as thirty day's notice), so it's a good idea to check your local Small Claims Court for the rules in your area.

If, as the defendant, you are served fewer than the required days before your trial appearance, you may either go ahead with the case or ask that it be delayed. Still, it's a good idea to show up at the proper time to make this claim.

In computing the number of days to see if correct service has taken place, most states count the day of the court appearance but do not count the day the service is accomplished. Weekends and holidays *do* count.

Serving a Corporation

If a corporation is a defendant in your lawsuit, you must serve your papers on an officer of that corporation—the president, vice president, secretary, or treasurer. You may also usually serve the corporation by serving the secretary of state.

You can find out who the officers are by calling the corporation and asking.

Proof of Service

The court must be informed whether proper service has been completed. If you have elected to use the mails, the certified or registered mail receipt, which should be placed in the hands of the Small Claims Court clerk, fulfills this requirement.

However, if you have not used the mails, you must file a Proof of Service with the court clerk after proper service has been accomplished. This document, which must be returned to the clerk's office before the trial, is usually signed by the person who actually made the service. In many cases it must be notarized.

Note to defendant: To file a counterclaim, you may be required to complete a Claim of Defendant and file it with the Small Claims Court clerk. Then you will have to serve it on the plaintiff (using the same methods discussed earlier), usually at least five days prior to the court appearance date.

Five Most Commonly Asked Questions

1. *How expensive is it to file in Small Claims Court?*

   Costs vary from state to state. However, the range is from $5 to $25. In some states this includes mailing fees. The only other court cost is a small fee, usually under $20 dollars, for serving papers on the defendant.

2. *Once I choose a court date, is it impossible to change it?*

You may change the court date by getting in touch with the Small Claims Court clerk and asking for a change. But remember, it is your responsibility to then inform the defendant of that change.

3. *I was named as a defendant in a Small Claims suit. I cannot make the appearance date but would like to contest the dispute. Is there anything I can do about this?*

First contact the plaintiff and tell him or her that the date is inconvenient and try to come up with a new date that is acceptable to both of you. If this doesn't work, contact the Small Claims Court clerk, state your problem, and let him or her provide you with a new court date.

4. *Once I institute a Small Claims suit, is it my responsibility to see that papers are served on the defendant?*

Indeed it is. You can do this in any one of several ways, including hiring a law enforcement officer or professional process server, using a friend or relative, or using the mail (registered or certified letter). But no matter which way you use, you must provide the court with proof of service.

5. *I was named a defendant in a Small Claims suit but I would like to make a counterclaim. How do I do this?*

Go to the Small Claims Court and fill out a defendant's counterclaim document. But remember, you are responsible for serving this paper, in the same way that the plaintiff is responsible for serving the Plaintiff's

Claim. In some states you are permitted to file the counterclaim the day you appear. If you do this, you have the advantage of surprise over the plaintiff, who may not be aware of or prepared for your action.

5

PREPARING YOUR CASE

Once you've received the date and time of your court appearance, it's time to begin to pull your case together.

Perhaps the first question you might ask yourself is: Do I need an attorney? The answer, in the large majority of cases, is no. However, it might not be a bad idea to consult with an attorney first. Although there will be a small fee for the consultation, it might pay large dividends. An attorney can help you organize your case, formulate questions to ask your adversary, and even shape a strategy you can follow.

Although most states do allow you to bring an attorney into Small Claims Court, it is usually not necessary. The rules and procedures of the court have been purposely made simple enough for you to master, and if you're concerned about a particular point of law as it relates to your case, it's far more economical to hire an attorney on an hourly basis and simply consult with him or her before-hand. Also, some Small Claims Courts now have free legal advisor programs under which you may consult with an attorney or paralegal who has volunteered his or her services. If this service isn't available in your state, you may, if your income is low enough, qualify for free legal assistance through the legal aid office.

Don't be afraid to appear in court without an attorney at your side. The court is interested in the facts of the case, and the judge will make the decision based on the applicable theory of law.

Once you appear in front of the judge or an arbitrator, perhaps the most important thing you should remember is to present your case as rationally and logically as you possibly can. Don't get excited. Be prepared to answer any questions the judge might have straightforwardly and without unnecessary embellishment.

Make sure that you have all the appropriate papers, such as bills, contracts, statements from witnesses, accident reports, estimates for costs of repair or replacement, photographs, and letters to or from your adversary (this would include your original demand letter). At the proper time, you will be asked to hand these "exhibits" to the clerk, who will in turn relay them to the presiding judge.

Remember, when it comes to these kinds of items, it's best to keep them as simple as possible. Greater volume doesn't necessarily translate into greater chances of winning your case.

When speaking, try not to repeat yourself. Remember, the judge sees many cases each day. The easier you make it for him or her to weigh the evidence, the more likely it is that he or she will look more kindly on your case.

It's much the same when it comes to witnesses. If you have any, make sure that they are at the court at the proper time and are prepared to testify to what you want them to. Make sure that what they have to say is relevant to your case. Also, they must have *firsthand* information concerning your case. It's not enough for them to say they heard "such and such."

Choosing and Preparing Witnesses

When it comes to witnesses, here are a few rules of thumb.

• Make sure your witnesses know the nature of your

case as well as the arguments they are likely to hear from your opponent.

- Make sure your witnesses know what you want them to say. This will necessitate a certain amount of coaching (this does not mean having them lie for you; rather it's a way of organizing their thoughts so they may present them more effectively). Never bring in a witness if you don't know what he or she is going to say. Needless to say, surprises at the time of the trial are not something you should look forward to.
- Don't bother bringing a "hostile" witness to court, that is someone who either does not wish to testify for you or finds the whole idea of testifying abhorrent. This kind of witness can only do damage to your case.
- Don't let your witnesses ramble. Good preparation should do away with this problem.
- You may pay an expert witness a reasonable fee to appear on your behalf (a subpoenaed witness is also entitled to a small fee), but under no circumstances should any other money change hands. If it does and this fact comes up in court, it could quickly sink your case.

Subpoenaing Witnesses and Documents

If necessary, most states will allow you to subpoena a witness (that is, require their presence) if he or she lives within a particular distance from the court. (This distance varies, so check your local rules.) In order to do this, pick up a subpoena form from the Small Claims Court clerk, fill it out, and then have it served on your witness. However, it's not a good idea to subpoena someone you haven't notified first or someone who does not wish to appear for you, because this may turn your own witness against you.

A person who is subpoenaed is entitled to a small witness fee if he or she requests it. This fee will probably be recoverable if you win your case.

Although only rarely in Small Claims cases would it be necessary for you to do so, you can also subpoena documents. For this you will need what's known as a Subpoena Duces Tecum. To get one you will have to prepare an affidavit stating why you need the particular papers, then take it to the Small Claims Court clerk who will have to issue the subpoena. (The procedure for a subpoena will vary—check with your local court.) This kind of subpoena must be directed to the person who is actually in charge of the documents you seek. For instance, if you need the financial records of a small business, you would normally direct your Subpoena Duces Tecum to the bookkeeper (be sure to obtain the name of the bookkeeper who is to be served).

Written Statements

Sometimes it may be impossible for a witness to appear in court on your behalf. If so, you may present a written statement from the witness. In it, he or she should state the date of the event in question; whether he or she was an eyewitness to the incident; whether he or she is an expert witness, along with any relevant expert opinion; and any other facts that have some bearing on your case. These statements should be notarized.

Once again, it's wise to make the statement as brief and to the point as possible.

Note that some courts will not accept this kind of testimony because it is not subject to cross-examination. Nevertheless, it's certainly worth presenting in the event that the judge might accept it.

Some Small Claims Courts will even accept testimony by telephone if your witness has a good enough excuse for not being in court. This might include illness, being out of state, or being unable to take time off from a job.

If you do wish to use telephone testimony, clear it with the court clerk beforehand. Don't be vague about it. It's a good idea to have a letter from your witness explaining why he or she can't appear in court and what he or she intends to testify about.

If it is allowed in your local court, a conference call can be set up so that your witness can testify and be heard by all present.

Physical Evidence

You may also want to present physical evidence, such as an item of clothing that was destroyed, an object that was damaged, or even a set of X rays.

If you do decide to present physical evidence, make sure that it reflects positively on your case and that it is not so cumbersome that it defeats your purpose. If the item is too large to bring into court, you might consider substituting photographs instead. It's not quite as dramatic, but it will usually do the job.

How to Deal with
Your Adversary

Before you get into court, it's a good idea to try to figure out the arguments your adversary is likely to use. This way you can try to counter them effectively.

Once you get into court, the best way to treat your adversary is with respect. Don't interrupt him or her. Don't get into any personal arguments. Simply direct your case to the judge. If your adversary has a hair-trigger temper or is inflammatory in any way, your calmer demeanor is likely to work for you.

Five Most Commonly Asked Questions

1. *Am I better off bringing an attorney with me to Small Claims Court?*

   As Small Claims Court was established so that the average citizen could have a forum to decide disputes without having to spend huge sums of money and tie up long periods of time, the benefits of being represented by an attorney are minimal. The judge decides each individual case on the facts presented to him or her, and you can present these facts at least as well as and perhaps better than an attorney. You might consult an attorney for advice or for specific pointers as to the appropriate theory of law, but beyond that, Small Claims cases are one time when representing yourself doesn't necessarily mean that you have a fool for a client.

2. *May I bring witnesses into Small Claims Court?*

   Yes, but if you do make sure they can present firsthand testimony that is relevant to your case. The last thing you want is someone who comes in and rambles on and on without adding any pertinent facts to bolster your side. For this reason, be sure to meet with your witnesses before their appearance to brief them on your case and tell them what you expect them to testify to. Also, it's a good idea not to have too many witnesses. The last thing a judge wants to see is a parade of witnesses, most of whom may add little or nothing to your case.

3. *Can I subpoena a witness to appear in Small Claims Court?*

   In most cases the answer is yes. But you should use subpoenas judiciously. You don't want to haul a witness into court who doesn't want to be there, because the chances are that his or her hostile attitude won't do your case much good.

4. *I have a witness I'd like to appear for me in court, but he lives several hundred miles away and can't make the trip in. Is there anything else I can do?*

   You may get a written statement from your witness, giving the date of the event in question and all the pertinent facts, as well as an explanation of why he or she can't appear in court. Or you may set up a conference phone call. Check your local court rules to see if this is acceptable.

5. *I have an upholstered chair that was ruined beyond repair when it was sent out to be cleaned. Can I bring the chair in as evidence?*

   If you can get it through the door, you can bring it in. If not, you may have to let a photograph do the talking.

6

WHEN YOU'RE THE DEFENDANT

Instead of being the plaintiff in a Small Claims Court action, you may find yourself as the defendant. If that's the case, this chapter will help you decide what your courses of action are.

Appearance in Court

If the plaintiff has acted as he or she should, it should not come as a total surprise that you're being sued (you should have been alerted by the plaintiff's demand letter, assuming that one was sent). But you can't actually be certain that someone has taken legal action against you until you receive service of the Plaintiff's Claim.

At this point there are several things you can do. First of all, the service may have been improper, for any one of a number of reasons. Perhaps the papers were simply left at your doorstep rather than delivered to you personally; or perhaps you weren't given the proper amount of time before your scheduled court appearance.

If this happens, rather than show up on the scheduled date and explain to the judge that the service was improper, it's best to contact the court clerk and ask for a continuance—a postponement until a more convenient time. However, you should make certain that your request is granted. Otherwise, a judgment may be entered against you.

If nothing is wrong with the service and you have no defense against the charge, you might choose simply not to appear. But if that's the case, the judge will enter a default judgment against you for the entire amount that you're being sued for, plus filing fees and costs. If you do appear, you might be able to persuade the judge to give the plaintiff a lesser amount.

If for some reason the plaintiff doesn't appear, which is rare, the judge will usually dismiss the case. In some instances this means that the plaintiff could have another shot at you. Check your local rules to see how this failure to appear applies to you as the defendant.

If you decide not to fight the plaintiff's claim but are not in a position to pay the award all at once, it's a good idea to appear in court and explain the situation to the judge. In some states it is within his or her power to allow you to pay the judgment in reasonable installments.

Compromise

Upon receiving the Plaintiff's Claim, you may decide there is some merit in the case, but that the suit is for too much money. If this is so, you may be able to come to some kind of settlement before going to court. Contact the plaintiff and see if you can work something out.

If you are able to come to some kind of mutually acceptable settlement, make sure you get it in writing. This should include an agreement from the plaintiff that he or she will drop the pending lawsuit against you.

Litigation

You may decide that you are in the right and prefer to fight the dispute in court. In this case, you must either appear in court at the scheduled day, time, and place, or you may request a continuance (first speak to the plaintiff to find a mutually convenient date; if that doesn't work, contact the court clerk).

If you decide to fight back, then you must prepare your case in precisely the same way the plaintiff would, gathering the appropriate papers, statements, witnesses, and so on.

You may also decide that you want to file a counterclaim against the plaintiff arising out of the same incident. If you do, you must go to the Small Claims Court clerk and fill out the appropriate papers, which you will then have to serve on the plaintiff.

Vacating Dismissals

Perhaps you failed to appear in court because you were never apprised of the action against you. As a result of your nonappearance, the plaintiff was awarded a default judgment.

In some cases you, as the defendant, may be able to convince the court to set aside or vacate that default judgment. This is a difficult though not impossible task. It's up to the individual judge, but if you have a good excuse, such as that you were not served or that you were suffering from an illness that made it impossible for you to appear, you might be able to get the judgment set aside. But remember, this just means that you will have to appear in court at a later date to answer the Plaintiff's Claim.

In some states, if you do decide to ask the court to set aside a default judgment, you must obtain the proper form from the clerk's office. Also, in many jurisdictions to vacate a default judgment you must show improper service and a meritorious defense.

Five Most Commonly Asked Questions

1. *I've just been served with papers stating that I'm being taken to Small Claims Court. What if I just ignore this?*

If you ignore the papers and fail to appear at the scheduled court hearing, the judge will most likely institute a default judgment against you for the amount of the plaintiff's claim. If a specific amount is not requested, a hearing might be held to determine damages.

2. *I'm being taken to Small Claims Court. Although I admit that the plaintiff does have a good case, I don't think the amount he's suing for is justified. Is there anything I can do?*

You can certainly try to come to some kind of compromise before the case comes to court. If that doesn't work, be prepared to state your case for a lower monetary award when you appear in court. The judge can always lower the plaintiff's figure if your argument is convincing enough.

3. *I'm being taken to Small Claims Court and I want to fight the case. Is there anything I have to do?*

Just appear in court on the scheduled day and time, prepared to present your case the best way you can, which means bringing witnesses and the appropriate documents.

4. *I'm being sued over an accident where I sustained damage to my car due to the plaintiff's negligence. Do I have to institute a separate suit to recover?*

No. Just file a defendant's counterclaim by filling out the proper forms, which are available from the Small Claims Court clerk. Once these papers are filled out, they must be served on the plaintiff within the proper time limits. Your respective cases will be heard by the judge at the same time. Of course, if the amount of your counterclaim is large enough, you might consider consulting an attorney first about bringing a separate action in a different court.

5. *I was sued in Small Claims Court and missed the court date because I was unexpectedly sent out of town. A default judgment was entered against me. Is there anything I can do to reverse that?*

You can ask the judge to set aside the default judgment, but you have to convince him or her that your reason for not showing up was a valid one.

7

PRESENTING YOUR CASE
IN COURT:
THE HEARING

Rules of Behavior

If both plaintiff and defendant appear at the appointed date
and time, ready to plead their respective sides, the chances
are, due to the usual court backlog, they will have to wait
some time until the clerk finally calls their case.

Once the case is called the judge will begin by asking
each party to identify him- or herself. Once this is accomplished, the plaintiff will be asked to state his or her case
briefly.

If you are the plaintiff, it is at this point that you should
explain to the judge what the dispute is all about and then
briefly tell why you think you deserve to recover. Only
rarely should this opening statement exceed five or six
minutes. If it does, you're probably taking too long to state
your position.

Here you should also take the opportunity to present any
relevant evidence, such as photographs, documents, bills,
and so on, that will strengthen your case. Hand them to the
clerk (who will then give them to the judge), and explain
what they are and why they are relevant. Also, inform the

judge as to the presence of any witnesses. The judge will determine whether to hear their testimony immediately or after the defendant has presented his or her case.

When you've completed your presentation, the judge may want to ask you some questions.

Then the judge will give the defendant his or her chance. If you are the defendant, remember to be patient and not interrupt the plaintiff, even if you think he or she is lying or misrepresenting the facts. You will only run the risk of alienating the judge and, besides, you will get your chance to refute the plaintiff's arguments. You might like to take notes during your adversary's presentation, so that when your turn comes you won't forget what you want to respond to.

As the defendant, first tell your side of the dispute and then refute any statements made by the plaintiff that you consider false.

Following are a few general tips that may be helpful to both plaintiff and defendant.

- Try not to read your statement. It is advisable to bring notes and refer to them as often as necessary, but all in all, you stand less of a chance of the judge nodding off if you keep your presentation fresh and conversational.
- It's always a good idea to stand when addressing the judge. It not only shows respect, but it may also enhance your presentation. Don't worry about showing nervousness. The judge knows that you're in a stressful situation and doesn't expect you to act as if you've spent your life in a courtroom.
- Again, we can't stress too much the advantage of being brief. This doesn't mean that you should leave anything out. It just means that you ought to be economical in what you say and avoid repeating yourself.

- Don't speak directly to your adversary. Don't interrupt, or make faces or gestures while he or she is speaking. Rest assured, you will get your chance to get your point across.
- If your case necessitates bringing diagrams or the like (as it might in a motor vehicle case), make sure they're clear and to the point. If you can't draw with reasonable legibility, have someone else do it for you beforehand. If you need a chalkboard, one will be made available. Use it, but again, only if you can draw well enough so that the judge can understand what you're trying to diagram.
- Be respectful. Don't antagonize the judge with a haughty or arrogant attitude. Judges are only human and if they take a dislike to you, it might somehow influence their decision.
- If you're the plaintiff, after you've completed your presentation, don't forget to inform the judge of any expenses you've incurred. Although you may not recover for taking time off from work, for any necessary copying of documents, or for the expense of hiring someone to watch your children, you may recover your court filing fee, the cost of service, fees paid to witnesses you've subpoenaed, and the cost of obtaining any necessary documents.

Following are some of the most common kinds of cases you're likely to find in Small Claims Court, along with some suggestions as to how you might handle them.

Money Cases

By far the most common kinds of cases heard in Small Claims Court involve money owed either for a service rendered or for the repayment of a loan.

If you are the plaintiff, you must first prove that the money is actually owed and that it has not been repaid.

If you are owed money, it's a good idea to sue as soon as it looks as if you're not going to receive it otherwise. If you wait too long not only will you risk running afoul of the statute of limitations, but you also risk the chance of the debtor either filing bankruptcy or disappearing.

If you have a written contract or note that you can produce in court, you're in pretty good shape. Producing proof of any payments that have already been made (this acknowledges that there was, indeed, a debt), along with documentation of any interest charged, will also appreciably strengthen your case.

In the case of debts based on oral contracts, you may have a tougher time of it if the defendant claims, for instance, that he or she never borrowed the money or purchased the goods. You must come up with some kind of documentation proving that the debt exists or with a credible witness who can testify that the defendant does actually owe you the money. You may also show the existence of a debt by establishing a pattern of behavior on the part of the defendant that proves that a debt exists. For instance, in the case of a loan, if you can produce canceled checks for even one payment, this can show that the defendant knew that a debt was owed, because he or she had begun payment on it.

If, on the other hand, you are a defendant in such a case, you might be able to prove that, for instance, you never received the goods or services for which it is claimed you owe a debt. Or perhaps the goods you received were defective; your argument might be that you ought not be obliged to pay for whatever it was you received. In this case, your proof could be the defective product itself, or if this is not possible, photographs that graphically illustrate the problem.

Automobile Cases

Another common kind of case heard in Small Claims Court has to do with damage done to an automobile or other vehicle. In most circumstances these cases would be handled by insurance companies. However, if the amount is small (less than the deductible), or if you prefer not to get your insurance company involved lest it mean a change in your rates, you may choose Small Claims Court to bring your action. If your case falls into this category, there are several things you can do to handle it properly.

First, you must determine whether you've suffered damage that translates into a monetary loss. If, as the result of an accident or the improper repair of your car, it fails to work the way it should, and it will cost you money to put it back in good working order, then you have suffered a monetary loss.

The next thing you must prove is that negligence played a role in the damage to your car. Sometimes, as when your automobile is hit by another automobile or object, this is rather easy. Other times, as in trying to prove that your mechanic improperly repaired your automobile, it's somewhat more difficult. But if you decide to sue, you must deal effectively with this question.

You do this by collecting evidence relevant to your case. Perhaps it's a defective part, statements from other mechanics, witnesses, or relevant photographs.

To this end, you should have your automobile checked by a reliable mechanic, one who can give you an estimate of the damage.

Other problems concerning motor vehicles include purchasing a new car that turns out to be a lemon. Most of the states have enacted some kind of "lemon law" to protect the consumer, but if the manufacturer refuses to comply by repairing the defect or replacing the car, you may have to take the company to court.

Another problem that crops up is the purchase of used cars from dealers. Occasionally, certain aspects of the car are misrepresented. If the dealer refuses to make good on repairs or a refund, you may have to sue.

And finally, you may experience problems with an automobile you've purchased from a private party. Perhaps the person misrepresented the condition the car was in or conveniently "forgot" to inform you of some "slight" problem with the engine.

Automobile accidents are another popular category of cases you'll often find in Small Claims Court. Usually, this does not include personal injury, but rather damage to a vehicle, which would include a motorcycle or bicycle.

If your automobile has been damaged in an accident, you should make the claim against the negligent driver of the other vehicle, even if you weren't at the wheel at the time. If the driver of the car that caused the damage is not the registered owner of the vehicle in question, you should also bring suit against the owner, as both of them are liable. If you're not sure if the driver is also the owner, just contact your local Department of Motor Vehicles, provide them with the license plate number of the car, and they will furnish you with the information.

If there are any witnesses to the accident, make sure you contact them and either bring them into court or obtain a written statement from them. Although family members or friends who happened to be in the vehicle at the time are acceptable witnesses, it's always better to find someone who is impartial and therefore has nothing to gain from his or her testimony.

Another useful tool in vehicular accident cases is a police report, which is admissible as evidence in most Small Claims Courts. If such an accident report does exist, get a copy of it and bring it into court, as it might go a long way in helping to establish proof of your claim of the other driver's negligence.

It's also a good idea to visit the scene of the accident and take photographs or draw a diagram of the area so you can better explain to the judge the circumstances surrounding the accident. Photographs of the damage done to your vehicle may also be helpful, along with several estimates as to the cost of repair, or one certified paid bill if the work has already been completed. Remember, you are also entitled to recover the fair market value of anything in your car that was destroyed as a result of the accident as well as the cost to you of alternative transportation while your vehicle was being repaired (this must be only for a reasonable period of time, however).

As a defendant, you certainly have the right to question the plaintiff's figures. As proof that the defendant's estimates may be too high, you should provide estimates made by your own experts.

Landlord-Tenant Cases

Another category that often finds its way into Small Claims Court is disputes between landlords and tenants. A case may be filed by the tenant in an attempt to get a security or cleaning deposit returned, regarding rent control violations, or regarding the failure of the landlord to provide essential services. Or the landlord may file a claim to recover unpaid rent or for damage done to the rental property. In some rare instances, a landlord may even use Small Claims Court to evict a tenant from the premises.

The most common landlord-tenant dispute concerns the failure to return a deposit that is supposed to cover any damage repair or cleaning necessary when the tenant moves from the house or apartment. Because this area is often very subjective in nature (How clean should an apartment be left? What's considered damage to the apartment?), these kinds of cases are difficult to present. One thing you can do, however, before the fact, is to make a note of any damage in the apartment at the time you first move in. Take photographs, if that's possible. And do the same thing when you move out.

But regardless of what you do to protect your interests initially, in most states the burden of proof is still with the landlord to prove that the premises were left in a damaged or unclean condition.

If you feel your security deposit is being withheld unreasonably, you should begin with a letter to your landlord stating your position: that you left the premises in perfectly acceptable condition and that you expect the return of your deposit. Also mention that if you don't receive a response within two weeks, you will be forced to bring the matter to Small Claims Court, where in many states the landlord will also run the risk of being hit with "bad faith" punitive damages.

If this doesn't work, you must decide whether it's in your best interests to carry through on your threat.

In court, you should be able to show photographs of the apartment when you moved in, if you have them, and certainly when you moved out. If you have it, you should also produce a dated, signed, and witnessed list of the damages noted when you moved in. You might even produce receipts for cleaning supplies (or for a cleaning service, if you hired one) that performed the job when you moved out. Bring along any witnesses who can attest to the condition of the premises when you moved in and when you moved out. Also, bring a copy of your lease and the letter you sent to the landlord asking for the return of your money.

If you are a landlord suing in Small Claims Court to recover unpaid rent, then you should bring the lease with you, along with a list of the periods of time for which no rent was paid. Also, you should be prepared to counter any claims by the defendant that he or she did not receive the basic services contracted for or that the premises were uninhabitable.

Another possible area of litigation occurs when a tenant leaves an apartment with several months remaining on a written lease. Landlords, especially small homeowners, may choose to sue for the balance of the rent due on the lease. However, the court usually requires the landlord to mitigate the damages, that is, show that steps have been taken to re-rent the premises.

Clothing Cases

If you're claiming damage to clothing, you must remember that unless the item was brand-new, you are probably not going to receive full value in order to replace it, but rather the fair market value at the time the damage was done. So, even though that coat you purchased a year ago cost you $750, there's no way the court will award you more than $400 or $500, depending on how persuasive you can be as to what should be considered the fair market value.

When you appear in court you should have the damaged clothing with you to show the judge. You should also bring proof of the original purchase price (this may be a receipt from the store, a credit card slip, or even a statement from the store attesting to the price), along with the date the item was purchased.

If you're suing on damage caused by a cleaning establishment, you'd better make sure that the cleaner was actually responsible for the damage, rather than some defect in the clothing. If there was a defect, you would be better advised to go after the manufacturer.

Property Damage Cases

The fellow who lives in the apartment above you left the water running in his bathroom. It seeped down through the ceiling and caused a flood that spread to your bedroom, destroying your carpet. The costs of cleaning up and replacing the carpet came to $650.

The is one kind of scenario concerning property damage that might wind up in Small Claims Court. In these kinds of cases you should be prepared to show receipts for the clean-up, proof of the value of the carpet, proof that it was destroyed beyond use, and estimates for a new carpet of comparable value (you can't go out and order a carpet three times as expensive and expect the judge to go along with it).

Again, in dealing with these kinds of cases, it's important to pinpoint blame. If, for instance, the flood was a result of faulty pipes, it would be the landlord you'd go after, not your upstairs neighbor. Of course, you also have the option of suing both parties in the same action and then letting them fight over the question of who is liable.

Consumer Service Suits

Often people contract for services that are either never performed or performed so poorly that the consumer would have been better off if they'd never been performed at all.

In such cases you should, as usual, begin with a letter to your adversary, stating that you never received what you contracted for. If your adversary either fails to return any money you've already paid or refuses to perform the service, you may choose to take him or her to court.

If you do, bring any contract you might have with you. If the contract was an oral one, bring any witnesses who might have been present when the deal was struck. If the job was begun but never completed, bring photographs or witnesses. Also, bring proof of payments made and an estimate of how much it would cost to complete the service that you originally contacted for.

If the job was completed but so incompetently that you

had to go out and have it done over again, bring proof of the added cost and perhaps a statement from whomever you hired to do the job over again as to the conditions he or she found when work was undertaken.

Five Most Commonly Asked Questions

1. *I'm a plaintiff in a Small Claims Court and I'm afraid I've overprepared. For instance, I can bring six witnesses into court. Should I do this?*

   Put yourself in the judge's position. Would you like to hear six witnesses testifying to essentially the same thing? Likely not. Unless each of your witnesses can enlighten the judge in a way that's necessary for him or her to come to a conclusion that's favorable to you, you're best off keeping your presentation as brief as possible. If you're afraid that your case isn't strong enough with only one or two witnesses, get written statements from the other four and be ready to show them to the judge if it's necessary (remember, written statements may not be accepted by some courts because they cannot be cross-examined).

2. *There are very bad feelings between me and the man I'm suing and I'm afraid I'm going to lose my temper in court. Can this hurt my case?*

   In an ideal world, if the facts are on your side, it shouldn't. But unfortunately, we don't live in an ideal world. If you allow your emotions to get the better of you, there's always the risk that the judge, who is, after all, human, might be subtly influenced against you. Why take the chance? Ignore your adversary and concentrate on presenting your case as well as you possibly can.

3. *Damage was done to my property when it was hit by an automobile. The man driving the car was not the registered owner. Whom do I sue?*

In your suit you should name both the driver and the registered owner of the car.

4. *My landlord refuses to return the cleaning deposit on my rental apartment. I say I left the apartment cleaner than when I took it. He says I didn't. As I don't have any photographs of the apartment when I first took it, how can I prove my case?*

Take photographs of the way the apartment looks now. If you've returned the keys to your landlord, request access by the super. Also, if you have any witnesses who can attest to the way the apartment looked when you first moved in, bring them into court. And if you reported any damage during the term of your lease that was the responsibility of the landlord but was never repaired, make a note of that. Otherwise, it's probably just a matter of your word against the landlord's.

5. *I brought a dress in to be cleaned and it was ruined in the process. The dress is several years old and it wasn't that expensive when I bought it. But it is a favorite of mine and I would like to recover something for it. How much can I sue for?*

Unfortunately, you can't recover for sentimental value. Assuming that the cleaner was indeed responsible for the damage, you can only recover the fair market value of the dress. In this case, by your own admission, the dress isn't worth much, perhaps not even as much as the cost of bringing the case in Small Claims Court. You should take this into consideration before you proceed.

8

THE AFTERMATH: DECISION AND APPEAL

The Judgment

In most instances (though not all), if the defendant fails to appear at the appointed court date, the judge will immediately enter a default judgment in the plaintiff's favor. In some states the judge will hold an inquest at which the plaintiff testifies to his or her damages, and then the default is entered. Otherwise, in most states after the case is heard, the judge's decision will be mailed to the plaintiff and defendant within a few weeks. This is not because it takes that long for the judge to arrive at a decision, but rather to avoid any potential unseemly courtroom scenes. Occasionally, however, the judge will give his or her verdict at the time, along with a brief explanation as to how and why he or she arrived at this decision.

If you are the winner in the case, you are known as the *judgment creditor,* and your adversary, the loser, is referred to as the *judgment debtor.*

If the judgment goes against you and you can't afford to pay the entire amount of the award at once, you may request a time payment. You may make this request at the time of the appearance (you should make this clear at the end of your presentation to the judge, for instance, "If you do find against me, I would like to arrange to pay over a period of time,") or after the court's decision is announced.

If you prefer to make your request after you leave court, the best thing to do is first contact the judgment creditor and see if you can work out a payment schedule. If you can, get it in writing so that you're protected. If you can't, you should see the Small Claims Court clerk and ask that you be allowed to appear in front of the judge again to arrange a payment schedule.

Once your judgment is paid, whether all at once or in installments, the judgment creditor must file what is known as a Satisfaction of Judgment form with the court. If you are the judgment debtor, make sure this is done after you've made full payment. If this form is not filed, then the judgment will remain on your credit record as being unpaid and may reflect negatively on your ability to obtain credit in the future. Send a letter to the judgment creditor demanding this Satisfaction of Judgment be filed. If it is not filed within a certain number of days (which varies according to the rules established by your local Small Claims Court), then you have the right to recover all actual damages you might sustain as a result of this failure to file.

If, for some reason, you fail to receive a Satisfaction of Judgment form, there are other acceptable items of proof of payment. These include a canceled check or money order made out by the debtor after the date of the court awarded judgment for the full amount of the judgment; a cash receipt for the full amount of the judgment signed by the creditor; a statement signed by the debtor under penalty of perjury avowing that the creditor has been paid in full the amount of the judgment plus costs. An explanation should also be included to the effect that the creditor has been requested to file a Satisfaction of Judgment but refuses to do so, or can't be found, and that the enclosed documents, which

T 471—Notice of Appeal.   COPYRIGHT 1973 BY JULIUS BLUMBERG, INC., LAW BLANK PUBLISHERS

Blumbergs
Law Products

Index No.

NOTICE OF APPEAL

PLEASE TAKE NOTICE, *that the above named*

hereby appeal(s) to

from the   *of the*
Court   *in this action, entered in the office*
of the Clerk of said Court

on the   *day of*   19

and from each and every part thereof.
Dated:

Yours, etc.,

Attorney(s) for   *and Appellant*

To

Attorney(s) for   *and Respondent;*

State of New York, County of   **ss.:**

being duly sworn, deposes and says; that deponent is not
a party to the action, is over 18 years of age and resides
at
That on the   day of   19
deponent served the within notice of appeal on

attorney(s) for
herein, at his office at
during his absence from said office
strike out either (a) or (b)
(a) by then and there leaving a true copy of the same
with
his clerk; partner; person having charge of said office.
(b) and said office being closed, by depositing a true copy
of same, enclosed in a sealed wrapper directed to said
attorney(s), in the office letter drop or box.

Sworn to before me this
day of   19

State of New York, County of   **ss.:**

being duly sworn, deposes and says; that deponent is not
a party to the action, is over 18 years of age and resides
at
That on the   day of   19
deponent served the within notice of appeal on

attorney(s) for
at
the address designated by said attorney(s) for that purpose
by depositing a true copy of same enclosed in a postpaid
properly addressed wrapper, in — a post office — official depository under the exclusive care and custody of the United
States Postal Service within New York State.

Sworn to before me, this
day of   19

Index No.

𝕹𝖔𝖙𝖎𝖈𝖊 𝖔𝖋 𝕬𝖕𝖕𝖊𝖆𝖑

Attorney(s) for Appellant

Office and Post Office Address

*Service of a notice of appeal of which the
within is a copy admitted this
day of   19*

Attorney(s) for Respondent

may include a check or money order, constitute evidence that the judgment creditor has received payment of the award.

The Appeal Process

Many, but not all, states allow either side to appeal a Small Claims Court judgment (some do not allow the plaintiff to appeal if he or she loses). In some states the losing defendant may appeal to a formal court, if this is done promptly.

Some states, such as Hawaii and Connecticut, do not allow any kind of appeal, while New York State allows an appeal of a judge's decision, but not of one made by an attorney-arbitrator (in New York, hearings take place more quickly if an attorney-arbitrator is acceptable to the plaintiff; if the plaintiff or defendant prefers, however, he or she may wait until a judge is available).

In some states either the plaintiff or defendant can appeal and the case will be heard over from the beginning. In other states only the defendant may appeal, but if he or she does, the case is heard from the beginning.

In almost half the states, an appeal can be made only on the basis of a question of law, not on the facts of the case. This means that the party appealing must argue that the judge misinterpreted the law, not the facts.

Before you begin the appeal process, first obtain a copy of your state's Small Claims Court appeal rules. Each state has its own rules regarding the number of days—anywhere from ten to thirty—after the original decision in which an appeal must be filed. The fee to appeal is usually somewhat higher than the fee paid to initiate the case.

On pages 65 and 66 is a facsimile of a Notice of Appeal.

Rather than taking place in Small Claims Court, your appeal will be heard in a formal court. As such, you are entitled to be represented by an attorney. However, attor-

Blumberg Law Products B 242—Whole or Partial Satisfaction of Judgment. Blank Court 8-87

© 1975 BY JULIUS BLUMBERG, INC., PUBLISHER, NYC 10013

COURT

COUNTY OF _____

Index No. _____

Plaintiff(s)

against

SATISFACTION OF JUDGMENT

Defendant(s)

WHEREAS, a judgment was entered in the above entitled action on _____ 19___
in the _____ Court of _____ County of _____
in judgment book _____ page No. _____ in favor of _____

and against

for the sum of $ _____ which judgment was docketed on _____ 19___
in the office of the Clerk of the County of _____ in judgment book _____ page No. _____

and said judgment has been _____ paid and the sum of $ _____ remains unpaid.
AND it is certified that there are no outstanding executions with any Sheriff or Marshal within the State
of New York,
THEREFORE, _____ satisfaction of said judgment is hereby acknowledged, and the said
Clerks are hereby authorized and directed to make an entry of _____ satisfaction on the docket of
said judgment.

Dated: _____

_____
The name signed must be printed beneath

STATE OF NEW YORK, COUNTY OF _____ ss.:

On the _____ day of _____ 19___ , before me personally came

to me known and known to me to be the
in the above entitled action, and to be the same person _____ described in and who executed the within satisfaction
of judgment and acknowledged to me that _____ he executed the same.

State of

County of { ss.:

On the   day of   , nineteen hundred and
before me personally came
to me known, who, being by me duly sworn, did depose and say that   he resides at No.

that   he is the   of

the corporation described in, and which executed, the foregoing instrument; that   he knows the seal of
said corporation; that the seal affixed to said instrument is such corporate seal; that it was so affixed
by order of the board of   of said corporation; and that   he signed his
name thereto by like order.

State of

County of { ss.:

On the   day of   , nineteen hundred and
before me personally came
personally known to me and to me known to be a member of the firm of

and to me known to be the person described in and who executed the foregoing satisfaction of judgment
in the firm name of   and   he acknowledged
that   he executed same as the act and deed of said firm for the uses and purposes therein mentioned.

Index No.

COUNTY OF   COURT

Plaintiff(s)

against

Defendant(s)

Satisfaction of Judgment

Attorney(s) for

Office and Post Office Address

neys cost money and because you are still suing for a relatively small amount of money, it might not make sense to hire outside help. Even if your opponent is represented by counsel, you are not necessarily at a disadvantage because the appeals court still follows the informal rules of the Small Claims Court. Thus there is no reason you can't also represent yourself at the appeal stage.

Although you might be more comfortable appearing before a judge, a few states do permit jury trials on appeal. Refer to your local Small Claims Court appeal rules to see if your state is one of these.

Five Most Commonly Asked Questions

1. *How long will it take to get the judge's decision on my case?*

   Some judges will render their decision immediately, explaining why they found the way they did. More frequently, however, you will receive the court's judgment by mail within two or three weeks of your appearance.

2. *I am on the wrong end of a $2,500 judgment in a Small Claims Court case. I can't possibly afford to pay all that at once. Is there anyway I can pay it off in installments?*

   Yes. If you didn't think to bring it up with the judge at the time the case was heard, you should immediately contact the judgment creditor and try to work out some kind of payment schedule. If you are successful in your plea, make sure you get this in writing. In some states if, for some reason, your creditor behaves unreasonably and refuses to accept periodical payments, you can contact the Small Claims Court clerk and ask to appear before the judge again to discuss paying off your debt in installments.

3. *I was taken to Small Claims Court three years ago. I lost the case and promptly paid off my debt to the judgment creditor, but I never received a Satisfaction of Judgment. Now I have applied for a credit card and I find that the judgment against me is still on my record, as if I never paid it off. Is there anything I can do rectify this?*

You can usually get a Satisfaction of Judgment document if you present to the court proof that you paid off your debt. This may consist of a canceled check or money order for the full amount of the judgment (with a date that coincides with the time of the judgment), or, if you paid in cash, a receipt signed by your judgment creditor. You should also provide a signed statement avowing that you have paid the full amount plus costs and that the enclosed documents constitute evidence that your payment was made.

4. *I was the plaintiff in a Small Claims case and the judgment went against me. Can I appeal?*

Each state has its own set of rules as to the appeal process. Most allow the plaintiff to appeal, but many do not. Check your local rules.

5. *Is the appeal process an expensive one?*

Usually the filing fee is $50 or under. This is more expensive than filing in Small Claims Court, but still not an unreasonable amount.

9

HOW TO COLLECT
YOUR JUDGMENT

You may think that once the judge rules in your favor your troubles are over. But in many cases your trouble has just begun, because now you have to collect the money owed you.

Many people are under the impression that the court will see to it that you are paid what you're owed. Unfortunately, this is not the way things work. It's *your* responsibility to get your money, but there are several options open to you.

The first thing you can do is to contact the judgment debtor and *politely* ask for your money. Having an official judgment does not mean you don't have to adhere to the amenities. Obviously, you're more likely to get your money if you don't antagonize the person you're trying to collect from.

In most cases a simple letter reminding the person that you have a judgment against him or her and giving a reasonable amount of time to forward the money will do the trick. However, if it doesn't, you will have to resort to other tactics.

In most states you may not resort to any official collection methods until after a specified time period, which runs from the date that your notice of entry of judgment was mailed (check your local rules for the precise number of days and the method for accomplishing this, in case it is not done automatically by the courts). But once this period has passed, several options are available to you.

Methods of Collection

If your judgment debtor refuses to pay your money, you may hire a collection agency. However, as these kinds of agencies charge up to 50 percent of what they can collect, it doesn't make much sense to go this route. In effect, then, you will become your own collection agency.

If you know where the judgment debtor works, you are allowed, under federal and state laws, to obtain up to 25 percent of the person's net wages weekly in order to satisfy a debt.

If you know where the judgment debtor banks, you can order a sheriff or marshal to levy on a bank account. This will allow you to get whatever the account contains, up to the amount you're owed, at the time of the levy.

Because every state has what are called *exemption laws*, other property, such as houses, furniture, and clothing, are, up to a point, untouchable. Consequently, the only other assets you can use to satisfy the debt are a motor vehicle in which the equity is far in excess of the exemption amount allowed in your state, real property other than that resided in by the debtor, and the receipts of an operating business.

Wages, Bank Accounts, Pensions, and Retirement Benefits

In order to get a levy on someone's wages or property, you must first obtain what's called a Writ of Execution or Notice to Judgment Debtor. This is not difficult once you have your Small Claims judgment. Simply obtain the form from the Small Claims Court clerk and fill it out. You will also have to pay a small fee.

Once you've received your Writ of Execution, give it and several copies (depending on the number of assets to be seized) to the local sheriff or marshal in the county in which the judgment debtor's assets are located (where he or she banks or works). Instruct the marshal or sheriff as to what should be collected and exactly where it is located. You must also be prepared to pay the collection fee (this varies from county to county). You must take this action shortly after receiving the writ, because it expires anywhere from within 60 to 180 days.

You may hire the sheriff or marshal by letter, but be sure to include all the relevant information as well as the appropriate fee.

In a number of states you are also entitled access to money that is held in banks in individual or self-employment retirement plans. You would go after these funds the same way as you would for money held in any regular bank account.

As for either private company and state or local government retirement plans, you must wait until the funds are actually paid to the employee.

Payroll checks issued by the federal government and federal government pension and retirement benefits may not be levied against to satisfy any debts other than those for alimony and child support.

Real Property

In order to obtain a lien on the judgment debtor's real property, all you need do is record an Abstract of Judgment (you can get this document from the Small Claims clerk, who will fill it out for you) at each local county recorder's office where the debtor owns property. Pay the fee and

Blumberg Law Products T 426—Notice to judgment debtors.
CPLR 5222 9-87

© 1982 BY JULIUS BLUMBERG, INC., PUBLISHER
62 WHITE STREET, NEW YORK, N.Y. 10013

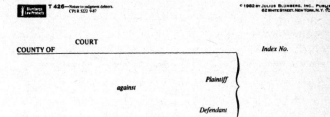

COURT

COUNTY OF _____

Index No.

Plaintiff

against

Defendant

NOTICE TO JUDGMENT DEBTOR

Money or property belonging to you may have been taken or held in order to satisfy a judgment which has been entered against you. Read this carefully.

YOU MAY BE ABLE TO GET YOUR MONEY BACK

State and federal laws prevent certain money or property from being taken to satisfy judgments. Such money or property is said to be "exempt". The following is a partial list of money which may be exempt:

1. Supplemental security income, (SSI);
2. Social security;
3. Public assistance (welfare);
4. Alimony or child support;
5. Unemployment benefits;
6. Disability benefits;
7. Workers' compensation benefits;
8. Public or private pensions; and
9. Veterans benefits.

If you think that any of your money that has been taken or held is exempt, you must act promptly because the money may be applied to the judgment. If you claim that any of your money that has been taken or held is exempt, you may contact the person sending this notice.

Also, YOU MAY CONSULT AN ATTORNEY, INCLUDING LEGAL AID IF YOU QUALIFY. The law (New York civil practice law and rules, article four and sections fifty-two hundred thirty-nine and fifty-two hundred forty) provides a procedure for determination of a claim to an exemption.

Dated

_____
*Creditor or Attorney(s) for Judgment Creditor
Office and Post Office Address*

State of New York, County of   **ss.:**

being duly sworn, deposes and says: that deponent is not a party

to this action, is over 18 years of age and resides at

That on   , 19   at   . M., at

deponent served the within Notice to Judgment Debtor to the judgment debtor therein named, by enclosing a copy of the
Notice in a postpaid sealed wrapper properly addressed to the judgment debtor

☐ **First Class**   to the last known residence address at
   Mail to
   Residence   and the deponent deposited the envelope in an official depository under the exclusive care and custody of
   the United States Postal Service within New York State.

☐ **First Class**   to the judgment debtor's place of employment at
   Mail to
   Place of
   Employment

   by depositing the envelope in an official depository under the exclusive care and custody of the United
   States Postal Service within New York State. The envelope bore the legend "personal and confidential" and
   did not indicate on the outside thereof, by the return address or otherwise, that the communication was from
   an attorney or concerned a judgment.

   The notice sent to the judgment debtor's residence had been returned.

☐ **First Class**   to (address)
   Mail to
   Other   and by depositing the envelope in an official depository under the exclusive care and custody of the United
   Address   States within New York State.

   The notice sent to the judgment debtor's residence had been returned and neither the residence address or
   the place of employment of the judgment debtor is known.

☐ **Personal**   by delivering a copy of the Notice on the judgment debtor personally; deponent knew the person so served to
   Delivery   be the person described as the judgment debtor therein.

Sworn to before me on   ....

                                            Print name beneath signature

then give the recorder the mailing address of the judgment debtor so that he or she can be notified. In effect, this means that when the judgment debtor wishes to sell that property, the buyer will find that title is clouded by your lien. The debt to you will have to be paid off before the property in question can change hands.

Business Assets

In a number of states, if the judgment debtor owns a business, you can have the sheriff or marshal visit that business and collect your debt from the cash available on the premises. In some states this function is filled by someone called a *keeper.* The keeper, who is usually a deputy sheriff or marshal, is assigned to remain at the judgment debtor's place of business for a "shift," which may range from eight to forty-eight hours. This keeper is mandated to take all money that comes into the business during that shift, until the debt is paid off. However, this is a costly method of collection, as fees for the keeper's time run high.

Note: Many states allow the judgment creditor to recover the direct costs incurred as a result of collecting the money due them. Check your local Small Claims Court rules to see if this is possible in your state and, if it is, how to go about it.

Five Most Commonly Asked Questions

1. *I've just received a judgment in my favor in Small Claims Court. Does the court collect the money for me?*

   No, you have to either do it yourself by writing a letter demanding payment as per your judgment or by engaging, for a fee, the sheriff or marshal in the county where the judgment debtor resides to collect the debt for you.

2. *The judgment debtor refuses to pay me my money. I know where he works and where he banks. Is there anything I can do?*

Yes, you may get a Writ of Execution from the Small Claims Court clerk, which will allow you to garnishee the judgment debtor's salary (up to 25 percent) or bank account.

3. *I have a judgment against someone who now claims that she does not have the funds to pay me. Is there anything I can do about that?*

Unfortunately, if the judgment debtor truly does not have the means to pay and has no attachable property (property that is nonexempt, that is), there is precious little you can do about it. This is something you should have checked on before you took the defendant to Small Claims Court. It would have saved you a good deal of time and trouble.

4. *I am a judgment debtor and cannot pay what I owe to the judgment creditor. I've recently lost my job, have virtually nothing in the bank, and have few assets other than the house in which I and my family live. Will I be forced to sell my house?*

In all states the house in which you reside (up to a certain value) is exempt, so you will not have to sell it. However, in many states the judgment creditor may put a lien on your house, which means that you may not sell it without paying off the amount that you owe. You may be able to make a deal with the judgment creditor, asking him or her to wait for the money until you're back on your feet again. If not, and the debt remains on your record, you will find it difficult to obtain credit in the future.

5. *I've spent a good deal of money trying to recover the judgment I received in Small Claims Court. Is any of this money recoverable?*

   In most states, yes. Speak to your local Small Claims clerk and ask him or her how to go about it.

Index